Julia But

Written by Melaina Faranda

PEARSON

Imagine living in the top of a giant tree for two years. Imagine never coming down from that tree to touch the ground ... Julia Butterfly Hill did just that. She did it to protect a 1500-year-old tree – and the ancient redwood forest around it – from a large logging company.
She endured extreme storms and cold.
She endured the loneliness of being apart from friends and family. She had to rely on other people who shared her cause. They sent up everything she needed to survive in buckets on a rope. Many people found it hard to believe Julia could love a tree so much that she'd give up everything to save it...

Julia Lorraine Hill was born on 18 February 1974. The first ten years of her life were spent on the road travelling with her family in a caravan. When she was six, a butterfly landed on Julia's finger while her family was out hiking. They nicknamed her Butterfly and even today she is known as Julia Butterfly Hill.

Julia's family eventually settled in a city in Arkansas in the United States. Julia grew up as an ordinary teenager. She finished school at sixteen, then worked as a waitress and restaurant manager. She wanted at that time, like most other people, to build a career, make money and own things.

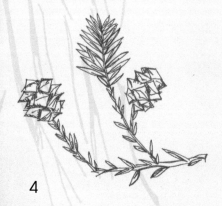

5

In 1996, when she was twenty-two, Julia was nearly killed when the car she was driving was hit by a drunk driver. In the accident, a steering wheel entered her head. It took a year for Julia to learn to walk and talk properly again. It was a time for her when she came to see life differently. She wanted, above all, to make a positive difference.

After her medical treatment had finished, Julia went on a road trip to California. When Julia first entered the ancient redwood forests, she claims she had a life-altering experience. She felt as if she had entered into a holy place. But only a few weeks later, she discovered this special environment was being destroyed. Julia was determined to save it. She wanted to save the forests. People protesting the logging of giant redwoods were tree-sitting to prevent a logging company from clear-felling the forest.

People in California continue to protest the logging of forests. In 2006, this tree-sitter set up a hammock high up in a redwood tree.

On 10 December 1997, Julia began her first
tree-sit. In the dead of the night, the protestors
sent provisions up the 55-metre, 1500-year-old
redwood they called Luna. It was midnight
when Julia finally put the harness on and
climbed up to the platform perch. The platform
that was to become her home for two years
and eight days!

At first, Julia thought she would be living in
Luna only for a few weeks. It was during her
time in Luna, she became convinced that
people should do more to try to protect
the environment. She made a promise that she
would not touch the ground again until she had
done everything possible to make the world
aware of the forest's plight.

Julia's new home was two small wooden platforms high up in the ancient tree. She sheltered under tarps. During the coldest, rainiest winters on record, she often had to stay wrapped up in a sleeping bag using only a small breathing hole. She was harassed by megaphones and all-night spotlights, as well as a helicopter creating high-speed wind blasts in the attempt to drive her down.

Julia, however, refused to give in.

Eight support team members below from the Earth First group made sure Julia had enough food and supplies, which she pulled up to her platforms with ropes. Julia used a single burner stove to cook on and a mobile phone to use for radio interviews. She also featured on cable television as an in-tree correspondent.

The tree became Julia's entire world. She learned to keep her feet sticky with sap to make climbing easier. She took time to come to observe everything about Luna, including the way rain droplets ran off the bark. She made the decision that if the hardship she went through brought further life for the 1500-year-old tree, it was worth it.

Two years and eight days after she had climbed Luna, Julia touched the ground for the first time. A deal had finally been made with the logging company to protect Luna with a 60-metre buffer zone.

When Julia's feet touched the ground, she curled into a ball and wept. People had been concerned she wouldn't be able to walk, but she skipped barefoot along the ground.

In an interview shortly after her descent from Luna, she said, "If we're going to make change in the world, the first thing we need to do is inform each other. The second thing we need to do is inspire each other to realise that we can make a difference; that our actions can change the world. One person can make a difference…"

Julia often speaks at charity events to help the environment. She travels the world speaking about her experiences.

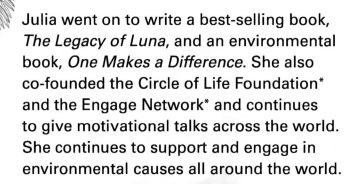

Julia went on to write a best-selling book, *The Legacy of Luna*, and an environmental book, *One Makes a Difference*. She also co-founded the Circle of Life Foundation* and the Engage Network* and continues to give motivational talks across the world. She continues to support and engage in environmental causes all around the world.

Footnote
The Circle of Life Foundation is a group that inspires people to respect all life and work for peace. *The Engage Network* stands for peace, justice, and caring for the environment.

Julia signs her book for fans at an Earth Day celebration.

Biography

A BIOGRAPHY is a story of a person's life written by another person.

How to Write a Biography

Step 1

Choose a person that you want to write about.
Think of some questions you want to ask the person.

QUESTIONS TO ASK:

When were you born?

What was your family life like?

What made you take on the role of a tree-sitter?

What sort of things did you experience?

How did you survive in the tree for over two years?

What did it feel like coming down, knowing that you had saved the tree?

What else have you been involved in?

Step 2

Interview the person and make notes.

Julia Butterfly Hill

Born 19 February 1974

First ten years spent travelling with family in a caravan

Had bad car accident at twenty-two

After treatment went to ancient redwood forest

Had life-altering experience in the forest

Decided to take part in protest to save trees

Step 3

Look at your notes and make a plan.

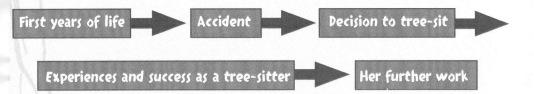

First years of life ➡ Accident ➡ Decision to tree-sit ➡

Experiences and success as a tree-sitter ➡ Her further work

Step 4

Use your plan to write the biography.

Step 5

Check your biography.

Can you add anything to make it more interesting?
Can you use time lines, sketches, photographs...?
Have you left anything out?
Can you take anything out that is not important?

Remember

If the biography is about a person who lived long ago or in a far-off place, use your library or the Internet to find out information about them. Then you can use the same steps to write up their biography.

Guide Notes

> **Title: Julia Butterfly Hill**
>
> **Stage:** Advanced Fluency
>
> **Text Form:** Biography
>
> **Approach:** Guided Reading
>
> **Processes:** Thinking Critically, Exploring Language, Processing Information
>
> **Written and Visual Focus:** Portrait Pictures, Press Photographs

THINKING CRITICALLY (sample questions)

- Look at the cover and title page. What form of writing do you think you will see in this book?
- Julia Butterfly Hill was a protester who fought for environmental causes. What might you expect to see in this book?
- Look at pages 2–3. Why do you think the author asks the reader to imagine living in the top of a tall tree for two years without coming down?
- How do you think Julia might have dealt with the loneliness of being separated from family and friends?
- Why do you think Julia made the choice to tree-sit? Do you think tree-sitting is an effective way to protest and save a tree? What reasons can you give to support your opinion?
- Look at pages 4–5. What inferences can you make about Julia as a person so far?
- Look at pages 6–7. What inferences can you make about why the accident made Julia see life differently?
- Do you think Julia would have gone on to be a tree-sitter if she hadn't had the accident? Why or why not?
- What do you think the author meant by the term *holy place?*
- Look at pages 8–9. What inferences can you make about how the first weeks of tree-sitting influenced Julia's decision to stay on in the tree?
- Look at pages 10–11. Do you think the logging company's harassment of Julia was fair? Why or why not?
- Look at pages 14–15. Julia believed one person can make a difference? Do you think this is right? Why or why not?
- Why do you think the author chose Julia Butterfly Hill as the subject for this biography?
- What questions do you have after reading the text?
- Who would you recommend this biography to and why?